INNKEEPERS
& LIGHT SLEEPERS

INNKEEPERS
& LIGHT SLEEPERS

Seventeen New Songs for Christmas

by John L. Bell

WILD GOOSE PUBLICATIONS
Iona Community
GLASGOW

First published 1992

The Wild Goose is a Celtic symbol of the Holy Spirit.
It is the trademark of Wild Goose Publications.

© 1992 Iona Community/Wild Goose Publications
ISBN 0 947988 47 5

Wild Goose Publications
The Publishing Division of the Iona Community
Pearce Institute, 840 Govan Road, Glasgow G51 3UU
Scotland
☎ (041) 445 – 4561

Printed and bound by
The Cromwell Press, Melksham, Wiltshire

Contents

Introduction

One of my closest friends wrote in the last Christmas card he sent, "I'm fed up with Christmas. I just want to go somewhere quiet and think about the incarnation."

And who could blame him, when from early November until the New Year, Bing Crosby, The Salvation Army and King's College Choir vie with each other from supermarket to dentist's surgery in providing 'seasonal' music or muzak.

To say that there is nothing wrong with traditional Christmas carols is to be less than discerning. Some − perhaps the majority − are good. But there are some which tell patent lies about the nativity or about Jesus himself.

There is no biblical evidence to support the theory that 'snow had fallen, snow on snow' but there is substantial evidence to suggest that Jesus did not 'honour and obey' throughout all his wondrous childhood. What about him running away from his family when returning from Jerusalem?

There is also the temptation to depict the characters in the nativity story as less than full-blooded. Mary tends to be portrayed as anaemic, docile and constantly doting, not the kind of woman who could cope with a pile of dirty nappies. Joseph is sometimes depicted as spineless and the shepherds and wise men, perhaps too closely modelled on their Sunday-school nativity play stereotypes, lack either humour or surprise.

And in the midst of all this, the wonder, the confusion, the conundrum of the incarnation is hid behind the verbal equivalent of Victorian stained glass.

Now this is not an indictment of all carols, nor is it to suggest that what appear in this selection represents the answer.

But here, our hope is that sometimes by coming at the story from a different angle, or by allowing the characters to speak in a distinct way, it may be possible both to grasp the earthiness of the people in the Christmas story as well as the mystery of the incarnation.

With regard to distinct speaking, it should be noted that the two lullabies are not charismatic transcriptions – unless, of course, you regard Scots as a charismatic tongue. The earliest post-reformation carols in Scotland were in this language, which is still spoken in parts of the country, and they were set to local folk tunes.

There's no reason why all these songs should not be sung by congregations. Indeed, they all have. But for their best use, it is profitable to try to forge new musical relationships in a church, by deploying soloists, choir and congregation as co-actors in a drama, rather than have the congregation sit dumb while the 'trained singers' have their way, or have everybody sing everything and all end up mentally and physically exhausted.

Suggestions are given with each carol as to how it may be sung co-operatively, and we would encourage users to be adventurous in sharing the songs.

My personal thanks goes to my colleague, Graham Maule, who has helped shape these songs and has prepared the book for publication; to our secretary Maggie Simpson for working on the text, to Jeanne Fisher and Michael Lee for their care in producing the manuscript and typescript; and to the Wild Goose Worship Group who have nurtured these songs from conception to birth and who have recorded them on the accompanying cassette.

John L. Bell
September 1992

The Songs

14 My bonnie boy

MUSIC: 'Bonnie Boy' (JLB)

briskly

vs. 1&4 Oh Sar-ah she was nine-ty and I am scarce nine-teen; for

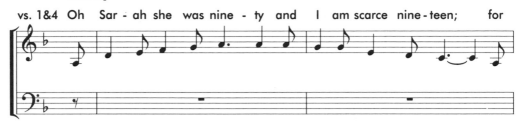

her the flower had with-ered, in me the leaf is green; to

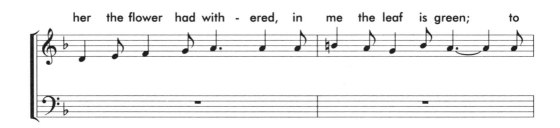

her was grant-ed laugh-ter, in me is plant-ed life, and my

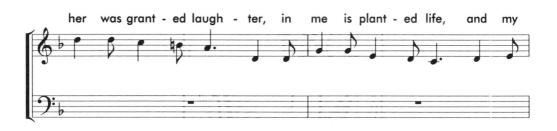

bon-nie boy will blos-som in the morn - ing. *fine*

(v.1 only) la la la la la la

16

child will bring me pleas - ure, my child will bring me grief; my

child will sow a whirl - wind and for - age like a thief. He'll

pro - test for the poor - est, he'll scat - ter all the proud, and my

d.c. for v.4

bon - nie boy will blos - som in the morn - ing.

1. Oh, Sarah she was ninety
    and I am scarce nineteen;
    for her the flower had withered,
    in me the leaf is green;
    to her was granted laughter,
    in me is planted life,
    and my bonnie boy will blossom in the morning.
2. His father is a carpenter,
    his father is a clown,
    his father is an angel
    who set on me a crown;
    a husbandman and harvester
    of holy, sensual seed,
    and my bonnie boy will blossom in the morning.

3. My child will bring me pleasure,
    my child will bring me grief;
    my child will sow a whirlwind
    and forage like a thief.
    He'll protest for the poorest,
    he'll scatter all the proud,
    and my bonnie boy will blossom in the morning.

4. Oh, Sarah she was ninety
    and I am scarce nineteen;
    for her the flower had withered,
    in me the leaf is green;
    to her was granted laughter,
    in me is planted life,
    and my bonnie boy will blossom in the morning.

It is hoped that this lively tune and atypical words may provide an antidote to the traditional depictions of Mary as a kind of anaemic Madonna. The song, which should never be allowed to drag and should never be accompanied, can be sung by soloist, by a congregation in unison or, as indicated here, in a choral arrangement.

18 He became poor

MUSIC: 'Flesh of our Flesh' (JLB)

gently

He be - came poor that we may be rich,

lov - ing the world and leav - ing his throne;

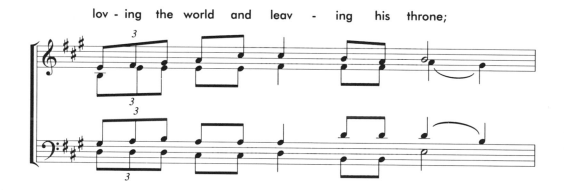

King of all Kings and Lord of all Lords,

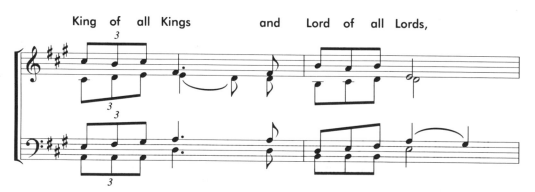

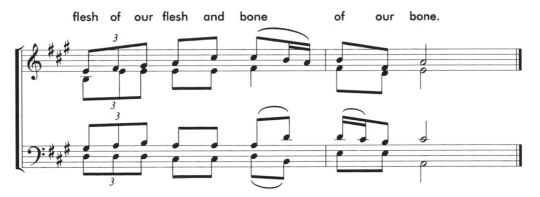

flesh of our flesh and bone of our bone.

He became poor that we may be rich,
loving the world and leaving his throne;
King of all Kings and Lord of all Lords,
flesh of our flesh and bone of our bone.

This is particularly appropriate as a gathering chant during the Advent season. Alternatively it may be used as a reflective response to intersperse short readings from the Christmas narrative.

20 Christmas is coming

MUSIC: 'Advent Ring' (JLB)

brightly

'CHRIST - MAS IS COM - ING', THE CHURCH IS GLAD TO SING AND

LET THE AD - VENT CAN - DLES BRIGHT - LY BURN IN A RING.

fine

v.1. The first is for God's pro - mise to put the wrong things right, and

bring to earth's dark - ness the hope of love and light.

d.c.

'CHRISTMAS IS COMING'
THE CHURCH IS GLAD TO SING
AND LET THE ADVENT CANDLES
BRIGHTLY BURN IN A RING.

1. The first is for God's promise
   to put the wrong things right,
   and bring to earth's darkness
   the hope of love and light.

2. The second for the prophets,
   who said that Christ would come
   with good news for many
   and angry words for some.

3. The third is for the Baptist,
   who cried, 'Prepare the way.
   Be ready for Jesus,
   both this and every day.'

4. The fourth is for the Virgin,
   who mothered God's own son
   and sang how God's justice
   was meant for everyone.

5. At last we light the candle
   kept new for Christmas day.
   This shines bright for Jesus,
   new-born, and here to stay.

(LAST CHORUS)   *CHRIST IS AMONG US.*
THE CANDLES IN THE RING
REMIND US THAT OUR SAVIOUR
WILL LIGHT UP EVERYTHING.

This is a teaching song for Advent which can be used as the Advent wreath has a new candle lit on each of the four Sundays and on Christmas Day. It is sufficient to have everyone sing the chorus with soloists, children or the choir taking the verses. Alternatively, from the 2nd Sunday in Advent onwards, the congregation can sing the 'old' verses and a child or adult soloist sing the new one as the relevant candle is lit. The song is suited to piano accompaniment.

22 Carol of the Advent

MUSIC: 'Stainer' (JLB)

with vigour

From a worn and wea - ry na - tion –

VE - NI IM-MAN - U - EL!

Where and when will come sal - va - tion?

VE - NI IM-MAN - U - EL!

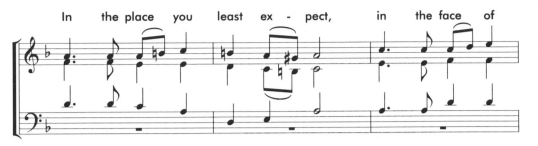

In the place you least ex - pect, in the face of

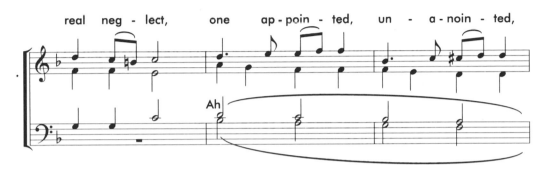

real neg - lect, one ap-poin - ted, un - a-noin - ted,

Ah

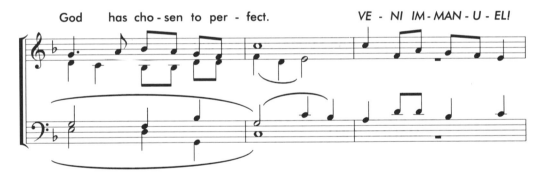

God has cho-sen to per - fect. VE - NI IM-MAN-U - EL!

VE - NI IM-MAN-U - EL! VE - NI IM-MAN-U - EL!

VE - NI IM-MAN-U - EL!

1. From a worn and weary nation –
     VENI IMMANUEL!
   Where and when will come salvation?
     VENI IMMANUEL!
   In the place you least expect,
   in the face of real neglect,
   one appointed, unanointed,
   God has chosen to perfect.
   VENI IMMANUEL! VENI IMMANUEL! VENI IMMANUEL!

2. To an unsuspecting mother –
     AVE MARIA!
   Why choose her and not some other?
     AVE MARIA!
   So that earth might be restored,
   flesh no longer be ignored,
   faith infected, love directed,
   God through woman be adored.
   AVE MARIA! AVE MARIA! AVE MARIA!

3. In the song of God's elected –
     MAGNIFICAT!
   Can the future be detected?
     MAGNIFICAT!
   God the proud will overthrow,
   worldly wealth will lose its glow;
   hunger halted, poor exalted,
   heaven appear through what we know.
   MAGNIFICAT! MAGNIFICAT! MAGNIFICAT!

4. Through the midnight air is seeping –
    GLORIA!
    Why such sound when most are sleeping?
    GLORIA!
    Thus shall strangers find their way
    where a simple family stay,
    recognising how surprising
    God appears when laid in hay.
    GLORIA! GLORIA! GLORIA!

5. Let the very earth cry glory,
    HALLELUJAH!
    Every tongue retell the story,
    HALLELUJAH!
    God no longer is confined
    out of sight and out of mind.
    Gone is distance and resistance;
    Christ is here in humankind.
    HALLELUJAH! HALLELUJAH! HALLELUJAH!

This is more a choral than congregational song, though it is easy to ask the
congregation to join in the exclamations in italics in each verse. Not all verses
need be sung. For example, if used prior to Christmas Day, the first three would
be sufficient.

26 No wind at the window

MUSIC: 'Columcille' (Irish trad. arr. JLB)

1. No wind at the window,
   no knock on the door;
   no light from the lampstand,
   no foot on the floor;
   no dream born of tiredness,
   no ghost raised by fear:
   just an angel and a woman
   and a voice in her ear.

2. 'Oh Mary, oh Mary,
   don't hide from my face.
   Be glad that you're favoured
   and filled with God's grace.
   The time for redeeming
   the world has begun;
   and you are requested
   to mother God's son.'

3. 'This child must be born
   that the kingdom might come:
   salvation for many,
   destruction for some;
   both end and beginning,
   both message and sign;
   both victor and victim,
   both yours and divine.'

4. No payment was promised,
   no promises made;
   no wedding was dated,
   no blueprint displayed.
   Yet Mary, consenting
   to what none could guess,
   replied with conviction,
   'Tell God, I say yes.'

This beautiful modal Irish tune provides a feeling of mystery appropriate to the
Annunciation to Mary. For its best effect, have a soloist or the sopranos sing
verses 2 and 3 while other voices hum the harmony. The congregation would then
be involved only in verses 1 and 4.

28 Justice in the womb

MUSIC: 'Against the Grain' (JLB)

lento

Not the fore - most of her gen - der, not the fin - est of her race; fav - oured now in re - pu - ta - tion, floun - dering then in deep dis - grace.

moderato

THOUGH FOR HER NO RIGHTS OR ROOM, THERE IS PRO - MISE IN THIS WO - MAN:

THERE IS JUS-TICE IN THE WOMB.

1. Not the foremost of her gender,
   not the finest of her race;
   favoured now in reputation,
   floundering then in deep disgrace.
       THOUGH FOR HER NO RIGHTS OR ROOM,
       THERE IS PROMISE IN THE WOMAN:
       THERE IS JUSTICE IN THE WOMB.

2. Cowed and occupied her country,
   dented was her people's pride:
   such a girl, in such a nation,
   could have been a soldier's bride.

3. Forced to make a tiresome journey,
   flanked by her redundant groom;
   all the brightness in her body
   longs to end the godless gloom.

4. All the power of heaven, contracted,
   gathers in this mother's pain:
   God, confounding expectations,
   sows her seed against the grain.

Like the incarnation itself, this carol is not without a sense of conundrum. Being in verse and chorus style, it is most effective when a solo voice acts as narrator for the verses and the congregation or choir sing the chorus in response.

30 And did it happen

MUSIC: 'Compelled by Angels' (JLB)

1. And did it happen
   that in a stable long ago,
   a weary couple,
   whom no-one seemed to know,
   should choose a manger,
   despite the danger,
   to hold and hallow the Lord below?

2. And did it happen
   that in the stillness of the night
   the woman laboured
   to let God see the light,
   and bathed and dressed him,
   breastfed and blessed him,
   the Word incarnate whose time was right?

3. And did it happen
   that news of this first reached the poor,
   compelled by angels
   to tiptoe to the door
   and see no trappings,
   just linen wrappings,
   a child for certain and God for sure?

4. And did it happen
   that all of this was meant to be,
   that God, from distance,
   should choose to be set free
   and show uniqueness,
   transformed in weakness,
   that I might touch him and he touch me?

To enable this song to be sung with the minimum of fuss, let a solo voice sing
verse one, another verse two, a third verse three and then the whole company can
sing verse four. It is particularly effective if the solo voices sing from among or
behind the congregation rather than performing in the front.

32 Look up and wonder

MUSIC: 'Mess and Manger' (JLB)

moderato

Look up and won-der at the stars which fa-scin-ate cre-
a - tion. Are these not fit to fill God's heart with
glad-ness and e-la - tion? Yet God for-sakes the
bound-less skies for earth and in-car-na - tion.

1. Look up and wonder at the stars
   which fascinate creation.
   Are these not fit to fill God's heart
   with gladness and elation?
   Yet God forsakes the boundless skies
   for earth and incarnation.

2. Look round at worldly wealth and skill,
   at intellect and labour.
   Are these not fit to handsel heaven
   and guarantee God's favour?
   Yet God forsakes what we pursue
   to meet the humblest neighbour.

3. Look down on makeshift dwelling place
   for animal or stranger.
   Is this not fit to distance God
   from trouble, dirt and danger?
   Yet God forsakes a better home
   to hallow mess and manger.

4. Christ must be cradled, not in stars
   or fame or worldly treasure.
   Instead God chooses those whose hearts
   hold things that none can measure.
   In justice, kindness, love and peace
   Christ finds his place and pleasure.

Of all the songs in this collection, this one most resembles a 'classical' hymn or chorale. It should be sung at a steady pace and is well suited to four-part harmony.

34 God immersed in mystery

MUSIC: 'Midwife' (JLB)

gracefully

God im - mersed in mys - te - ry, Lord of time and

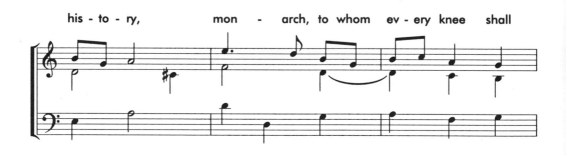

his - to - ry, mon - arch, to whom ev - ery knee shall

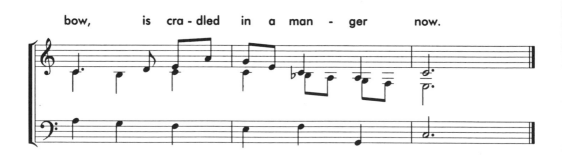

bow, is cra - dled in a man - ger now.

1. God immersed in mystery,
    Lord of time and history,
    monarch, to whom every knee shall bow,
    is cradled in a manger now.

2. God whose face was never seen,
    God whose hands were ever clean,
    nappied, and a price upon his brow,
    is cradled in a manger now.

3. God who made the planets move,
    midwife of both life and love,
    carolled by a cock or cat or cow,
    is cradled in a manger now.

4. God who gave the world its birth,
    God who promised peace on earth,
    Word, becoming flesh to keep that vow,
    is cradled in a manger now.

Essentially a solo song, this carol is best used on Christmas Day or the Sunday thereafter. It can be accompanied on piano or organ.

36 Funny kind of night

MUSIC: 'Lesser Things' (JLB)

not too slowly

Fun-ny kind of night, fun-ny kind of day, tax col-lec-tors, child in-spec-tors,

v.1,2,3 Fun - ny, fun - ny kind of

all in dis-ar-ray; fun-ny kind of day, fun-ny kind of night,

v.1 day, fun - ny, fun - ny
  2 night, all a - bove is
  3 day, while they hear poor

roy - al kings and les - ser things a - lign with dark and light. TO

v.1 kind of night,
  2 veiled in song: TO
  3 shep - herds sing:

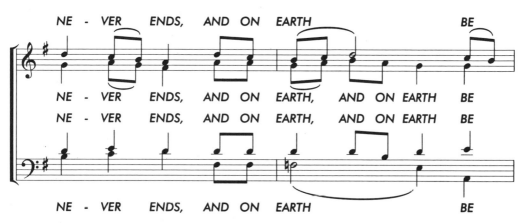

1. Funny kind of night, funny kind of day,
   tax collectors, child inspectors, all in disarray;
   funny kind of day, funny kind of night,
   royal kings and lesser things align with dark and light.

   TO GOD IN THE HIGHEST BE GLORY WHICH NEVER ENDS,
   AND ON EARTH BE PEACE AND GOODWILL TO ALL GOD'S FRIENDS.

2. Funny kind of day, funny kind of night,
   babies cry, traditions die and fear itself takes fright;
   country folk enquire what is right or wrong
   while above, in tongues of love, the sense is veiled in song:

3. Funny kind of night, funny kind of day,
   first begotten, half forgotten treasure lies in hay;
   wise men on the move wonder what to bring,
   while innkeepers and light sleepers hear poor shepherds sing:

Another choral song which requires for its best use, a four-part choir. The congregation can, of course, join in the chorus.

40 The pedigree

MUSIC: 'Pedigree' (JLB)

Not the power - ful, not the privi - leged,

not the fa - mous in the land, but the no - ones

and the need - y were the first to hold God's hand.

1. Not the powerful, not the privileged,
    not the famous in the land,
    but the no-ones and the needy
    were the first to hold God's hand.

2. Not a well established family
    with an heirloom christening shawl,
    but a homeless, wandering couple
    parented the Lord of All.

3. Not, at first, to little children,
    nor to those whose faith burned bright;
    but to adults, stalled in darkness,
    angels brought God's love and light.

4. God, determined to be different
    from the standards we think best,
    in his choice of friends and family,
    lets forgotten folk be blessed.

5. Not obsessed by our achievements,
    worldly wealth or family tree,
    may we, in and with God's chosen,
    find our fondest pedigree.

A four-part harmony hymn for Christmas Eve or Christmas Day. It is not necessary to teach the tune beforehand. Simply have a soloist or soprano voices sing the first three verses, with the other parts humming the harmony, and trust the congregation to join from verse 4. Sing accompanied or unaccompanied.

42 Ma wee bit dearie

MUSIC: 'Rory Dall's Port' (Scottish trad.)

like a lullaby

HUSH A BYE, MA WEE BIT DEAR - IE,

GREET - IN ON - LY MAKS YE WEAR - IE.

SLEEP SALL SMOOR YE SUNE OR LA - TER,

HAUD YER TEARS FOR THINGS THAT MAIT - TER.

HUSH A BYE, MA WEE BIT DEARIE,
GREETIN ONLY MAKS YE WEARIE.
SLEEP SALL SMOOR YE SUNE* OR LATER,
HAUD YER TEARS FOR THINGS THAT MAITTER.

1. In ma wame an angel wrocht ye,
    tae ma breist an angel brocht ye;
    heaven has kept ye weel attended,
    juist as God had aye intended.

2. Gowd is stour whaur ye are treasure,
    wealth is puir whaur ye are measure;
    tho yer hame is spare and shoddie,
    this was meant for Mary's lawdie.

3. Kings maun yet be stouned tae meet ye,
    wabbit folk be gled tae greet ye;
    a' the warld gaes tapsalteerie,
    spelter't wi' yer licht, ma dearie.

This is the first of two carols in Scots — the language in which the earliest carols appeared in Scotland after the reformation. And, in keeping with the ancient tradition, it is set to a folk tune. It has a gentleness about it which should not be overstressed, otherwise the pace will become slower and slower. Keep a regular beat throughout.

For those who cannot understand Scots, the following provides the gist of the chorus:

HUSH A BYE, MY LITTLE DEAR ONE;
CRYING ONLY TIRES YOU OUT.
SLEEP SHALL TOUCH YOU SOONER OR LATER,
SO HOLD YOUR TEARS FOR MORE IMPORTANT THINGS.

Ho ro ho ro

MUSIC: 'Blissin' (JLB)

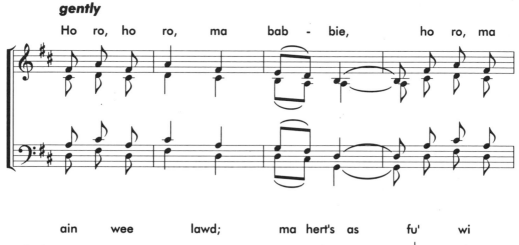

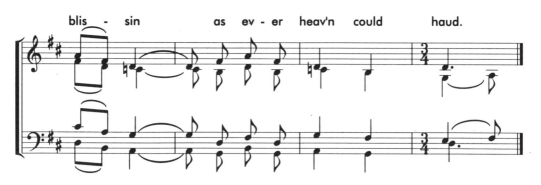

1. Ho ro, ho ro, ma babbie,
   ho ro, ma ain wee lawd;
   ma hert's as fu' wi blissin
   as ever heav'n could haud.

2. Yer mither loes yer faither,
   yer faither loes his wean;
   whit tho' we're waur than trochl't,
   God kens it maitters nane.

3. Ahint a boozie ludgin,
   forenenst whaur sodgers staun,
   ye kechle et ilk daunger
   an gie the warld yer haun.

4. I wance was sweirt tae hae ye
   for fear ye cam tae hairm;
   but mangst this queer clanjamfrie,
   I'm shure God's bared his airm.

5. Sae cam ye ben, puir crofters,
   An gaither roon fond kings;
   wha telt ye whaur tae fin us
   sall keep a haud o' things.

6. Ho ro, ho ro, ma babbie,
   ho ro, ma ain wee lawd;
   ma hert's as fu' wi blissin
   as ever heav'n could haud.

This lullabye can be sung by one, two or many voices. Unless skilled choristers are available, it is best to sing it in unison with piano or organ accompaniment. It is perhaps most effective when a female and male voice alternate, with everyone joining in the last verse.

Roughly translated, the chorus means:

HO RO, HO RO MY BABY,
HO RO, MY LITTLE MAN;
MY HEART IS AS FULL OF BLESSING
AS HEAVEN COULD EVER HOLD.

46 The aye carol

MUSIC: 'Aye Carol' (JLB)

like a lullaby

Who is the ba-by an hour or two old,

looked for by shep-herds far strayed from their fold,

lost in the world though more pre-cious than gold? This is God with us in

Je - sus.

last time

1. Who is the baby an hour or two old,
   looked for by shepherds far strayed from their fold,
   lost in the world though more precious than gold?
   This is God with us in Jesus.

2. Who is the woman with child at her breast,
   giving her milk to earth's heavenly guest,
   telling her mind to be calm and at rest?
   Mary, the mother of Jesus.

3. Who is the man who looks on at the door,
   welcoming strangers, some rich but most poor,
   scanning the world as if somehow unsure?
   Joseph, the father of Jesus.

4. Who are the people come in from the street,
   some to bring presents and some just to meet,
   joining their song to what angels repeat?
   These are the new friends of Jesus.

5. Will you come with me, even though I feel shy,
   come to his cradle and come to his cry,
   give him your nod or your *yes* or your *aye*,
   give what you can give to Jesus?

This carol was originally intended for children and can be effectively sung by
having an adult soloist ask the question in each verse, with children giving the
answer in the last line and all singing verse 5.

48 Simeon's song

MUSIC: 'Happit Awa' (JLB)

with dignity

'Take, Lord, and fold my life a - way; its pur - pose is ful -
filled. I clasp, ex - pressed in mor - tal clay,
all that your love has willed: this babe re - veals your
cost - ly grace to Is - rael and the hu - man race.'

words: Ian Fraser © Stainer and Bell, reproduced by permission;
music © 1992 Iona Community / Wild Goose Publications, Govan, Glasgow, Scotland.

1. 'Take, Lord, and fold my life away;
   its purpose is fulfilled.
   I clasp, expressed in mortal clay,
   all that your love has willed:
   this babe reveals your costly grace
   to Israel and the human race.'

2. May we, like Simeon, receive
   this new reality;
   and, living by it, now believe
   Christ came to set folk free,
   till kingdoms of the earth appear
   marked by God's rule and presence here.

This song derives from the *Nunc Dimittis* of Simeon, as contained in Luke Ch.2. v
29 – 32. It is a fitting anthem or vesper to a service of worship in the weeks
following Christmas.

50 Carol of the Epiphany

moderato

MUSIC: 'First Hand' (JLB)

I sought him dressed in fin - est clothes, where mon - ey talks and sta - tus grows; but power and wealth he ne - ver chose: it seemed he lived in pov - er - ty.

Voice A: 1. I sought him dressed in finest clothes,
where money talks and status grows;
but power and wealth he never chose:
it seemed he lived in poverty.

Voice B: 2. I sought him in the safest place,
remote from crime or cheap disgrace;
but safety never knew his face:
it seemed he lived in jeopardy.

Voice C: 3. I sought him where the spotlights glare,
where crowds collect and critics stare;
but no one knew his presence there:
it seemed he lived in obscurity.

Voice A: 4. Then, in the streets, we heard the word
which seemed, for all the world, absurd:
that those who could no gifts afford
were entertaining Christ the Lord.

ALL VOICES: 5. AND SO, DISTINCT FROM ALL WE'D PLANNED,
AMONG THE POOREST OF THE LAND,
WE DID WHAT FEW MIGHT UNDERSTAND:
WE TOUCHED GOD IN A BABY'S HAND.

This Epiphany Carol was written for the inaugural service of Glasgow's year as the City of Culture (1988). As indicated, it provides an alternative to *We Three Kings* in that it allows each of the three Magi to sing of their quest, and the congregation, in verse 5, to affirm what they discovered. It is best accompanied by an organ, making good use of flute stops.

52 The refugees

MUSIC: 'Refugees' (JLB)

Down the road run re-fu-gees, a child and fa-ther and mo-ther;

scared by what they've left be-hind and what they fear to dis-

words and music © 1992 Iona Community / Wild Goose Publications, Govan, Glasgow, Scotland.

1. Down the road run refugees,
   a child and father and mother;
   scared by what they've left behind
   and what they fear to discover.
   MOVE AND MOVE AND MOVE ALONG
   IN FAIR AND FOULEST WEATHER.
   STOP A BIT BUT DON'T STAY LONG;
   YOU MIGHT BE WAND'RING FOR EVER.

2. Hunted out like criminals
   and kept at distance like lepers,
   cursed and criticised by those
   who look and laugh at their papers.

3. At their back run twenty more
   and twenty thousand come later;
   twenty million follow these:
   each year the number gets greater.

4. Kampuchea, Vietnam
   and Mozambique provide them;
   folk like us with nothing to fear
   see fit to doubt or deride them.

5. Jesus and his parents fled
   from Herod's imminent danger;
   still he wanders with the crowds,
   a frightened, nationless stranger.

6. Who will help the refugees
   to cease their endless walking,
   while the ones who claim to care
   continue endless talking?

This carol is in the form of a protest-song, much the same as *Standing at the Door* by Sydney Carter. It requires a fairly forceful soloist and a piano accompaniment which keeps the music on the move. The congregation or choir can join in the chorus. If a drummer can be found to keep a steady beat throughout, so much the better.

Ten Golden Rules

for teaching new songs

1. Believe in the voice God has given you.
    It is the voice of an apprentice angel.

2. Believe in the voices God has given other people.

    Years of being told, and telling themselves, that they cannot sing can be redeemed by the confidence you show in other's abilities.

3. Teach only songs or harmony lines which you personally have sung in your bath or your bed.

    If you are uncertain about a song, that will be the first thing your 'trainees' detect.

4. Teach songs only at the appropriate time .... which is seldom if ever during a church service or even after the organ voluntary.

    The best time to teach is before anything happens, while people are still settling down. If they learn a new song then, they will recognise it as a familiar friend when used later in the service. **Never** antagonise a congregation by teaching a new song the minute it is to be used.

5. Always introduce a new song with enthusiasm; never with an apology.

    To tell a group of people that they 'have' to learn a new

song and that they 'might' pick it up is as appropriate as a tickling stick at a funeral.

6.   Use only your voice and hands to teach new tunes.

Human beings find it easier to imitate another human being than to copy a 12 string guitar, grand piano or pipe organ. They also pick up the pitch and rhythm of notes when they are signed in the air much more easily than when they are merely sung.

7.   When teaching, sing a bit worse than your best and always use your normal voice.

Remember, you are asking people to copy another person, not to be amused or threatened by the vocal dexterity of a real or would-be operatic superstar.

8.   Let the people know about the structure of a tune before you teach it, then teach it in recognisable sections.

e.g. if the 1st, 2nd & 4th lines are the same (as happens in many folk tunes), tell people that. Then you only have to teach two lines — the first (which is repeated later) and the second;

if the tune has a chorus, tell people that. Then teach them the chorus, and once they have it, you sing the verses while they sing the chorus, gradually picking up the verse tune en route.

but

if the tune does go fairly high, don't petrify people in advance by making a pained expression before the top note. Teach it down a key and later raise the pitch when people are familiar with it.

9.   When demonstrating:

a)   sing a verse or a verse & chorus over first

b)   teach a breath or two lines at a time, whichever is shortest

c)   don't teach a new phrase until the present one is recognisable

d)   sing the tune to 'la' if it looks too big a job to get words and music together at the first go

e)   after the song has been taught, you sing a verse through once, asking people to listen to you and correct, inwardly, their potential mistakes, if any

f)   ask everyone to sing the same verse together (if long verses) or the next verse (if short verses)

g) always thank and encourage those who are learning.

10. When using the song, already learned, in worship, try not to have all the people singing all the time.

Either get a soloist to do verse 1, thus refreshing everyone's memory; or get a small group or soloist to sing most of the verses and others join in the chorus, if there is one; or alternate verses between men and women, sides of the church or whatever. People enjoy a song much more when they don't have to sing all of it.

To get the right pitch, use a pitch pipe, chime bar or recorder.

To get people started, you sing the first line to 'la'. To get people singing well, you sit among them and if 'they' are expected to help lead the congregation to sing, think about positioning them not in the front of everyone, but behind or among other people.

To get the best from new songs, do not teach too many at one time.

Index of first lines

(alphabetical)